Index of Select Emergency Management Resources for North Carolina Local Governments

2026

Taylor Morris

The School of Government at the University of North Carolina at Chapel Hill works to improve the lives of North Carolinians by engaging in practical scholarship that helps public officials and citizens understand and improve state and local government. Established in 1931 as the Institute of Government, the School provides educational, advisory, and research services for state and local governments. The School is also home to a nationally ranked Master of Public Administration program; a Law, Government, and Public Service minor beginning in academic year 2026–2027; the North Carolina Judicial College; and specialized centers focused on community and economic development, information technology, and environmental finance.

The School is the largest university-based local government training, advisory, and research organization in the United States. Its current catalog of faculty scholarship features more than 1,000 books, manuals, reports, articles, bulletins, teaching resources, and other print and online content related to state and local government. Faculty at the School offer close to 300 courses, webinars, and specialized conferences each year for more than 15,000 public officials. The School also produces the *Daily Bulletin Online* each day the General Assembly is in session, reporting on activities for members of the legislature and others who need to follow the course of legislation.

Visit sog.unc.edu or call 919-966-5381 for more information on the School's courses, publications, programs, and services.

Aimee N. Wall, Dean
Jeffrey B. Welty, Senior Associate Dean for Faculty Affairs
Anita R. Brown-Graham, Associate Dean for Strategic Initiatives
Willow S. Jacobson, Associate Dean for Graduate Studies
Kara A. Millonzi, Associate Dean for Research and Innovation
Lauren G. Partin, Senior Associate Dean for Administration
Sonja Matanovic, Associate Dean for Strategic Communications and Partnerships
Matt Marvin, Chief Development Officer

FACULTY

Whitney Afonso	Kimalee Cottrell Dickerson	Kirsten Leloudis	John Rubin
Gregory S. Allison	Phil Dixon, Jr.	Adam Lovelady	Dylan Russell
Rebecca Badgett	Belal Elrahal	James M. Markham	Meredith Smith
Julie Beasley	Rebecca L. Fisher-Gabbard	Christopher B. McLaughlin	Daniel Spiegel
Maureen Berner	Jacquelyn Greene	Jill D. Moore	Carl W. Stenberg III
Kirk Boone	Timothy Heinle	Jonathan Q. Morgan	John B. Stephens
Mark F. Botts	Cheryl Daniels Howell	Taylor Morris	Elliot Stoller
Brittany LaDawn Bromell	Joseph L. Hyde	Ricardo S. Morse	Charles Szypszak
Melanie Y. Crenshaw	Colt Jensen	C. Tyler Mulligan	Shannon H. Tufts
Crista M. Cuccaro	James L. Joyce	Kimberly L. Nelson	Amy Wade
Leisha DeHart-Davis	Robert P. Joyce	Kristi A. Nickodem	Teshanee T. Williams
Shea Riggsbee Denning	Diane M. Juffras	Obed Pasha	Catherine Wilson
Sara DePasquale	Joseph Laizure	William C. Rivenbark	Kristina M. Wilson

Contents

Introduction and User Guide

This index provides a list of select potential resources for North Carolina local governments facing emergency-management-related issues. It is designed as a starting point for local government officials and staff who need help addressing an emergency-management challenge.

Scope of the Index

"Emergencies" and "Emergency Management" in This Index

To help users understand what materials are in this index and when the index might be helpful, reviewing the terms "emergency" and "emergency management" may be worthwhile. In North Carolina emergency management law, these terms have general meanings that may differ from what users imagine. So some resources that users might be seeking may not be in this index. And some resources might be included in this index that users did not expect.

Under North Carolina's Emergency Management Act (the EMA), *emergencies* are essentially "occurrence[s] or imminent threat[s] of widespread or severe damage, injury, or loss of life or property" coming from certain "natural or man-made…cause[s]."[1] *Emergencies* can also involve certain supply chain disruptions threatening provision or restoration of certain local government "essential services."[2] *Emergency management* involves efforts by governments and everyday people to address these types of emergencies before, at the time that, and after they are occurring.[3]

The index is designed to lay out resources for the types of emergencies and emergency management described in the EMA. The index is not attempting to provide resources related to anything a user might think of as an "emergency" in an everyday sense.

Audience

This index is aimed at providing resources for North Carolina local governments. References to a "user," "users," "you," "your," "readers," or similar terms are generally directed at North Carolina local government staff or officials (but in context, these terms or similar terms may refer to anyone using the index or someone else). Other people may consult the index if desired, but they are not the intended audience.

---

1. Chapter 166A, Section 19.3, Subsection 6 of the North Carolina General Statutes (hereinafter G.S.) (defining *emergency*).

2. *See id.*

3. *See* G.S. 166A-19.3(8) (defining *emergency management*).

Some Notes on Selection of Resources

Not every possible emergency management resource for North Carolina local governments is listed in the index. The index focuses mainly on free or low-cost resources that would be easily accessible with an Internet or telephone connection. The index also focuses mainly on resources that might be helpful across different emergencies, rather than resources specific to a particular emergency.

Additionally, while the index is designed to be helpful, the index is not updated in real time. Users should not assume that information listed or resources referenced in the index are current, correct, complete, comprehensive, and/or available. Online resources in particular might easily change, become outdated, move locations, be removed, or become inaccessible. Ultimately, users will be responsible for taking any appropriate steps to (1) verify information before use and (2) decide whether and how to use any information or resources.

Index Layout

The index lists emergency management resources alphabetically by topic (e.g., "contracts and procurement" or "public health").

It then divides the resources by types. It lists resource types for each topic in the following general order:

 **"First Stop" Resources (the first, local resources that local government staff or officials might consult for help with an issue)**

 **Select Training(s)**

 **Select Publication(s)**

 **Select Potentially Relevant Law(s)**

 **Other Miscellaneous Resource(s)**

 **State, Federal, Nonprofit, or Professional Organization Contact(s)**

 **School of Government Faculty**

Each listed topic may not have every single one of these resource types listed.

Note that because many topics overlap, resources may sometimes be listed under more than one topic. For example, information about the School of Government's Development Finance Initiative (DFI) is listed under "Community and Economic Development" and

"Development, Land Use, Planning, and Zoning." But when looking for resources, users may check in any section that they think may apply, to increase the chance that they find what they are seeking. Resources may not be cross-listed everywhere that a user might imagine.

In particular, note that "Grants" is a stand-alone topic in this index, and for brevity, the index generally lists resources focusing specifically on grants only under "Grants." But if a resource is not focused specifically on grants but just references grants or has some relevance to grants, the resource might be listed under another topic area.

Using the Index to Get Help

As a rule of thumb, users might consider (1) starting with "first stop" resources; then (2) consulting trainings, publications, potentially relevant laws, and other miscellaneous resources if they have not found what they seek; and then (3) reaching out to listed contacts if they still need help. However, this approach is just a suggestion. Each circumstance is different, and users may find that using these resources in a different order makes sense for their needs.

Starting with "First Stop" Resources

Generally, users might consider starting with their "First Stop" resources. "First Stop" resources will be (1) potential contacts or other resources from users' own local government unit and/or their county or (2) resources servicing their local area. On this second point, for instance, the "Utilities" section mentions local non-governmental utilities providers as potential resources. Local governments may be on the front lines of emergency management in any given emergency. Consulting local resources may be the most efficient way to find an answer or reach a solution.

Additionally, users may especially benefit from developing a habit of starting locally. By doing so, users can become familiar with local resources and establish or maintain connections with key local government emergency management personnel. These outcomes could be very helpful when dealing with an active emergency. During an emergency, users may feel overwhelmed and be under a high degree of stress. The emergency might also temporarily cut off access to outside resources, meaning users can only rely on local resources. If users already have a relationship with their local emergency manager and other key personnel, they will not need to try to find out who those people are, what they are like, and how to get in touch with them under such difficult circumstances. Users will already be familiar with working with these resources, rather than trying to establish a working relationship under the pressure of an emergency.

Using Trainings

Many emergency management issues might be addressed through taking a training. These trainings might be free, on-demand, or scheduled, and a training may even be offered by the entity that will evaluate how well you have performed the task on which you have been trained.[4] For instance, FEMA may offer trainings on doing FEMA-compliant purchasing.[5]

Consulting Publications

Your emergency management question may already be addressed through an existing publication. Users can consider reviewing publications in their topic area(s) of interest to see if their question already has an answer.

Reviewing Potentially Relevant Laws

Users might find an answer to their question through reviewing a relevant law. The index will list some potentially relevant laws in different topic areas. Again, though, the index does not necessarily list every law relevant to the topic or to anyone's specific situation. Further, links to the laws may not be to the official or current version of the law and are for reference only.

Using Other Miscellaneous Resources

For some topics, additional resources may exist that do not fit neatly into the other categories. The index has listed some of these resources that might be particularly helpful.

Reaching Out to State, Federal, Nonprofit, or Professional Organization Contacts

These contacts may be most helpful if users have not found an answer among the above resources. These contacts may also be particularly helpful if users have complex, detailed, or technical questions about state or federal emergency-management issues. In some cases, you may be able to contact someone from an entity that plays a role in evaluating your local government's compliance with the rule about which you were asking questions. For instance, you may be able to contact FEMA for assistance with evaluating whether you are doing contracting that complies with FEMA standards. See the "Contracting and Procurement" or "Grants" section for more details.

Reaching Out to School of Government Faculty

When Reaching Out Might Help Most

Reaching out to a School of Government faculty member may be most helpful if (1) the above resources did not answer a user's questions and (2) the user has a question about general rules or procedures for North Carolina local governments doing emergency management.

---

4. *See, e.g.,* Procurement Under Grants Training, https://www.fema.gov/grants/procurement/training (last visited May 13, 2026).

5. *Id.*

Which Faculty Member(s) to Potentially Contact

If a user's question relates to a listed topic area, contacting faculty members listed as contacts in that section of the index may be most efficient. Those faculty members have expertise in that general topic area and may be able to answer questions about that topic in an emergency management context.

Note that sometimes, a faculty member might not be listed as a contact for a topic area, even though a publication by that faculty member is included for that topic area. This outcome may happen when a faculty member's publication touches on the general topic area, but the faculty member is not necessarily a general subject-matter expert in that field. This situation may also happen when the faculty member no longer works for the School of Government (the index will attempt to note when a faculty member no longer is affiliated with the School of Government). Contacting the author of such a publication may be most helpful if (1) the author currently works for the School of Government and (2) users have specific questions about that publication. But contacting the faculty member(s) listed as contacts for the topic area instead may be more helpful if (1) the publication author no longer works with the School of Government or (2) users have a question in the general topic area but not related to a specific publication.

Contacting one of the faculty members under "General/Miscellaneous Emergency Management" would be most appropriate if users' questions do not relate to any of the other listed topics.

Faculty members will sometimes be listed with extra information about their specific areas of expertise when multiple faculty members are listed. That information should give users a better idea of which specific faculty member(s) they might wish to contact when multiple options are offered. Taking advantage of this information may save users time in getting to a good person to address the users' specific questions.

For a more detailed listing of faculty areas of expertise throughout the School of Government, you may use the faculty fields of expertise list: https://www.sog.unc.edu/sites/default/files/FINAL20250157%20FacultyExpertise_Jan2026_4.pdf.[6] Users can also find faculty by navigating to the School of Government's website, then going to About, then Faculty & Staff.[7] A link to the faculty expert list is on the School of Government website as well: https://www.sog.unc.edu/about/faculty-and-staff/.[8] Since this expertise list may be updated from time to time, the specific list linked above may become outdated. Visiting the School of Government's website may help users find a more updated list.

---

6. *See* FACULTY FIELDS OF EXPERTISE, JANUARY 2026, https://www.sog.unc.edu/sites/default/files/FINAL20250157%20FacultyExpertise_Jan2026_4.pdf (last visited May 13, 2026).

7. *See* FACULTY AND STAFF, https://www.sog.unc.edu/about/faculty-and-staff/ (last visited May 13, 2026).

8. *See id.*

Code Enforcement

"First Stop" Resources

- ▶ Your local government code enforcement officers
- ▶ Your local government permitting/inspections department
- ▶ Your county and/or municipal attorney
- ▶ Your county and/or municipal emergency manager
- ▶ Your local regulations

Select Publications

▶ **"Ordinance Enforcement Basics"**
Coates' Canons post by Trey Allen (former School of Government faculty member)[9]
Available here: https://canons.sog.unc.edu/2016/02/ordinance-enforcement-basics/

▶ **"Nuisance Abatement and Local Governments: What a Mess"**
Coates' Canons post by Richard Ducker (former School of Government faculty member)[10]
Available here: https://canons.sog.unc.edu/2011/06/nuisance-abatement-and-local-governments-what-a-mess/

▶ **"Nuisance Abatement and Local Governments: What a Mess—Part II"**
Coates' Canons post by Richard Ducker (former School of Government faculty member)[11]
Available here: https://canons.sog.unc.edu/2013/07/nuisance-abatement-and-local-governments-what-a-mess
-part-ii/

Select Potentially Relevant Laws

▶ **G.S. 160A-174**
General municipal ordinance-making power and nuisance abatement authority
Available here: https://www.ncleg.gov/enactedlegislation/statutes/html/bysection/chapter_160a/gs_160a-174.html

▶ **G.S. 160A-193**
Municipal summary abatement authority
Available here: https://www.ncleg.net/enactedlegislation/statutes/html/bysection/chapter_160a/gs_160a-193.html

▶ **G.S. 160A-205.6**
Municipal removal and disposal of abandoned vessels
Available here: https://www.ncleg.gov/EnactedLegislation/Statutes/HTML/BySection/Chapter_160A/GS_160A-205.6.html

---

9. *See* FORMER FACULTY MEMBER TREY ALLEN INVESTED AS MEMBER OF SUPREME COURT OF NORTH CAROLINA, https://www.sog.unc.edu/about/news/former-faculty-member-trey-allen-invested
-member-supreme-court-north-carolina (last visited May 13, 2026).

10. RICHARD D. DUCKER, https://www.sog.unc.edu/about/faculty-and-staff/richard-d-ducker (last visited May 13, 2026) (noting Professor Ducker's retirement).

11. *Id.*

▶ **G.S. 160A-303**

Municipal removal and disposal of junked and abandoned motor vehicles

Available here: https://www.ncleg.gov/enactedlegislation/statutes/html/bysection/chapter_160a/gs_160a-303.html

▶ **G.S. 160A-303.2**

Municipal regulation of abandonment of junked motor vehicles

Available here: https://www.ncleg.net/enactedlegislation/statutes/html/bysection/chapter_160a/gs_160a-303.2.html

▶ **G.S. 153A-121**

General county ordinance-making power and nuisance abatement authority

Available here: https://www.ncleg.gov/EnactedLegislation/Statutes/HTML/BySection/Chapter_153a/GS_153a-121.html

▶ **G.S. 153A-132**

County removal and disposal of abandoned and junked motor vehicles and abandoned vessels

Available here: https://www.ncleg.gov/EnactedLegislation/Statutes/HTML/BySection/Chapter_153A/GS_153A-132.html

▶ **G.S. 153A-132.2**

County regulation, restraint, and prohibition of abandonment of junked motor vehicles

Available here: https://www.ncleg.gov/EnactedLegislation/Statutes/HTML/BySection/Chapter_153A/GS_153A-132.2.html

▶ **G.S. 160D, Article 11**

Building code enforcement, including regulation of nonresidential structures and vacant building receivership

Available here: https://www.ncleg.gov/EnactedLegislation/Statutes/HTML/ByArticle/Chapter_160D/Article_11.html

▶ **G.S. 160D, Article 12**

Minimum housing codes

Available here: https://www.ncleg.gov/EnactedLegislation/Statutes/HTML/ByArticle/Chapter_160D/Article_12.html

 ## School of Government Faculty

▶ **Taylor Morris**

morris@sog.unc.edu

Community and Economic Development

"First Stop" Resources

▶ Your local community and economic development department
▶ Your county and/or municipal attorney
▶ Your county and/or municipal emergency manager

Select Publications

▶ **"Local Government as Lender: Emergency Loans for Small Businesses"**
Community and Economic Development in North Carolina and Beyond post by Tyler Mulligan
Available here: https://ced.sog.unc.edu/2020/03/local-government-as-lender-emergency-loans-for-small-businesses/

▶ **"Local Government Emergency Loans for Small Businesses: Contracting with Financial Institutions for Loan Administration"**
Community and Economic Development in North Carolina and Beyond post by Tyler Mulligan
Available here: https://ced.sog.unc.edu/2020/03/local-government-emergency-loans-for-small-businesses-contracting-with-financial-institutions-for-loan-administration/

▶ **"Local Government Support for Small Business Recovery and Reopening"**
Coates' Canons and *Community and Economic Development in North Carolina and Beyond* post by Tyler Mulligan
Available here: https://canons.sog.unc.edu/2020/08/local-government-support-for-small-business-recovery-and-reopening/

▶ **"Emergency Home Repair Loans: Local Government as Financial Bridge"**
Coates' Canons and *Community and Economic Development in North Carolina and Beyond* post by Tyler Mulligan
Available here: https://canons.sog.unc.edu/2024/11/emergency-home-repair-loans-local-government-as-financial-bridge/

▶ **"Vulnerability and Emergency Preparedness in Low-Income Communities"**
Community and Economic Development in North Carolina and Beyond post by John Cooper
Available here: https://ced.sog.unc.edu/2011/10/vulnerability-and-emergency-preparedness-in-low-income-communities/

 ## Other Miscellaneous Resource

Development Finance Initiative

The Development Finance Initiative (DFI) at the School of Government may be able to support local governments interested in development projects after an emergency, particularly those projects involving private investment.[12] More information about DFI's capabilities can be found at the DFI website: https://dfi.sog.unc.edu.[13]

 ## School of Government Faculty

▶ **Tyler Mulligan**
mulligan@sog.unc.edu

Contracting and Procurement

"First Stop" Resources
▶ Your local contracting/procurement/purchasing/finance department
▶ Your county and/or municipal attorney
▶ Your county and/or municipal emergency manager
▶ Your local contracting, procurement, or purchasing policies and procedures

Select Trainings

FEMA Procurement Disaster Assistance Team (PDAT) Procurement Under Grants Trainings

Live, Online Training Sessions

▶ **FEMA may offer scheduled training on procurement.**[14]
The schedule for this type of training is on the FEMA website.[15]
Available here: https://www.fema.gov/grants/procurement/training

---

12. *See* DEVELOPMENT FINANCE INITIATIVE, https://dfi.sog.unc.edu (last visited May 13, 2026).

13. *See id.*

14. *See* PROCUREMENT UNDER GRANTS TRAINING, https://www.fema.gov/grants/procurement/training (last visited May 13, 2026).

15. *Id.*

Self-Paced, Online FEMA PDAT Training

▶ **"Top Ten Mistakes When Purchasing Under a FEMA Award"**
FEMA estimates that this training will take a little over 30 minutes to complete.[16] A link to the training is located on the FEMA website.[17]
Available here: https://emilms.fema.gov/grantsmanagement/post-award/lessons/topmistakestoavoid/curriculum/1.html

Requesting a PDAT Training

In addition to taking the above offered trainings, local government staff may reach out to FEMA to arrange for a scheduled in-person or webinar PDAT training.[18] This option might be appropriate if the local government wants to cover a specific set of topics not covered in the other trainings, wants an in-person training option, or needs training at times other than those times that FEMA offers.

See the FEMA Procurement Under Grants Training page for more information: https://www.fema.gov/grants/procurement/training.[19]

Contacts for Scheduling a Training

Local governments can start the process of scheduling by emailing the PDAT team directly at fema-gpd-pdat@fema.dhs.gov.[20] Local governments could also consider reaching out to the FEMA Regional Office for North Carolina (North Carolina is part of Region 4, which includes several other states and Tribal Nations).[21] The Region 4 Regional Office general phone number is 770-220-5200, and its general email address is FEMA-R4-Info@fema.dhs.gov.[22] Additionally, local governments might reach out to The North Carolina Department of Public Safety's Division of Emergency Management ("North Carolina Emergency Management" or "NCEM").[23]

Select Publications

Select FEMA Publications

More Detailed Publications

▶ *Roadmap to Procurement Compliance*
Available here: https://www.fema.gov/sites/default/files/documents/fema_rsl-gpd_roadmap-to-procurement-compliance_202601.pdf

---

16. Top Mistakes to Avoid When Purchasing Under a FEMA Award, https://emilms.fema.gov/grantsmanagement/post-award/lessons/topmistakestoavoid/curriculum/1.html (last visited May 13, 2026).

17. *Id.*

18. *See* Procurement Under Grants Training, https://www.fema.gov/grants/procurement/training (last visited May 13, 2026).

19. *Id.*

20. *See* email from John Griego to Taylor Morris (June 23, 2025, 02:55 PM EDT) (on file with author).

21. *See id*; Region 4, https://www.fema.gov/about/regions/region-4 (last visited May 13, 2026).

22. Region 4, https://www.fema.gov/about/regions/region-4 (last visited May 13, 2026).

23. *See* email from John Griego to Taylor Morris (June 23, 2025, 02:55 PM EDT) (on file with author).

▶ ***Procurement Under Grants Policy Guide: Procurement Policy for Recipients and Subrecipients of FEMA Financial Assistance***
Available here: https://www.fema.gov/sites/default/files/documents/fena_gpd_procurement-under-grants-policy-guide_fiscal-year-2025.pdf

▶ ***Contract Provisions Guide: Navigating Appendix II to Part 200—Contract Provisions for Non-Federal Entity Contract Under Federal Awards***
Available here: https://www.fema.gov/sites/default/files/documents/fema_contract-provisions-guide-fy24.pdf

Shorter-Form FEMA Fact Sheets

▶ ***Purchasing Under a FEMA Award: Exigency or Emergency Circumstances***
Available here: https://www.fema.gov/sites/default/files/documents/fema_procurement-during-EE_factsheet_fy25.pdf. Older versions of this fact sheet are available on the FEMA website: https://www.fema.gov/grants/procurement/resource-library.[24]

▶ ***Purchasing Under a FEMA Award: Managing Fraud Risks***
Available here: https://www.fema.gov/sites/default/files/documents/fema_managing-procurement-fraud_factsheet_fy25.pdf

▶ ***Purchasing Under a FEMA Award: Prepare Before a Disaster***
Available here: https://www.fema.gov/sites/default/files/documents/fema_procurement-prepare-before-disaster_factsheet_fy25.pdf

▶ ***Purchasing Under a FEMA Award: Using the GSA Schedule***
Available here: https://www.fema.gov/sites/default/files/documents/fema_procurement-gsa_factsheet_fy25.pdf

▶ ***Purchasing Under a FEMA Award: 2024 OMB Revisions***
Available here: https://www.fema.gov/sites/default/files/documents/fema_pdat-omb-revisions_factsheet_fy24.pdf

Select School of Government Publications

▶ **"Emergency and Exigency According to FEMA"**
Coates' Canons post by Crista Cuccaro
Available here: https://canons.sog.unc.edu/2024/10/emergency-and-exigency-according-to-fema/

▶ **"Temporary Facilities for Government Operations Following a Disaster"**
Coates' Canons post by Crista Cuccaro
Available here: https://canons.sog.unc.edu/2024/12/temporary-facilities-for-government-operations-following-a-disaster/

▶ **"Performing a Cost or Price Analysis Under the Uniform Guidance"**
Coates' Canons post by Crista Cuccaro
Available here: https://canons.sog.unc.edu/2024/10/performing-a-cost-or-price-analysis-under-the-uniform-guidance/

▶ **"Emergency Procurement—When Is an Emergency Really an Emergency?"**
Coates' Canons post by Norma Houston (former School of Government faculty member)[25]
Available here: https://canons.sog.unc.edu/2011/06/emergency-procurement-when-is-an-emergency-really-an-emergency/

---

24. Resource Library: Purchasing Under a FEMA Award, https://www.fema.gov/grants/procurement/resource-library (last visited May 13, 2026).

25. *See* Faculty and Staff, https://www.sog.unc.edu/about/faculty-and-staff?page=1 (last visited May 13, 2026) (Norma Houston no longer listed).

Select Potentially Relevant Laws

▶ **2 C.F.R. 200.317–27**

General federal procurement regulations

Available here: https://www.ecfr.gov/current/title-2/subtitle-A/chapter-II/part-200/subpart-D/subject-group
-ECFR45ddd4419ad436d

▶ **G.S. 143-129(e)(2)**

State emergency bidding exception for certain construction, repair, and purchase contracts

Available here: https://www.ncleg.gov/EnactedLegislation/Statutes/HTML/BySection/Chapter_143/GS_143
-129.html

▶ **G.S. 166A-19.16**

State emergency bidding exception for certain purchase contracts

Available here: https://www.ncleg.gov/EnactedLegislation/Statutes/HTML/BySection/Chapter_166A/GS_166A
-19.16.html

○○○ Other Miscellaneous Resources

School of Government Local Government Purchasing and Contracting Microsite

The School of Government Local Government Purchasing and Contracting microsite (https://
www.sog.unc.edu/resources/microsites/local-government-purchasing-and-contracting/)
includes links to:

- Checklists, charts, and information on requirements related to contracts
- Sample procurement/property disposal forms
- Information on federal procurement requirements
- Information on potential School of Government purchasing courses
- A list of selected contracting publications
- Information on the School of Government purchasing listserv[26]

State Pre-Positioned Contracts

Debris Management

Information on the state's pre-positioned contracts for debris monitoring and debris removal
is on the North Carolina Department of Public Safety website at: https://www.ncdps.gov
/our-organization/emergency-management/disaster-recovery/public-assistance/debris
-management.[27]

---

26. Local Government Purchasing and Contracting: Tools, https://www.sog.unc.edu
/resources/microsites/local-government-purchasing-and-contracting/tools (last visited May 13, 2026).

27. Debris Management, https://www.ncdps.gov/our-organization/emergency-management/disaster
-recovery/public-assistance/debris-management (last visited May 13, 2026).

Mosquito Abatement
Information on the state's pre-positioned mosquito abatement contract is on the North Carolina Department of Public Safety website at: https://www.ncdps.gov/our-organization /emergency-management/disaster-recovery/public-assistance/mosquito-abatement-contract.[28]

State, Federal, Nonprofit, or Professional Organization Contact

FEMA Contracting Reviews
FEMA may offer some review of solicitation documents or executed contracts that are intended to comply with FEMA standards. FEMA may even be able to have a call with you to discuss your questions. To discuss accessing this potential service, email: fema-gpd-pdat@fema.dhs.gov.

School of Government Faculty

▶ **Crista Cuccaro**
cuccaro@sog.unc.edu

Development, Land Use, Planning, and Zoning

"First Stop" Resources
▶ Your local planning/zoning/development department
▶ Your county and/or municipal attorney
▶ Your county and/or municipal emergency manager
▶ Your local development, land use, planning, and zoning rules and regulations. Your local government may keep those rules and regulations in a land development ordinance, a unified development ordinance (UDO), and/or other parts of your local government code.

Select Publications

Select School of Government Blog Posts

▶ **"Adjusting Development Regulations for Disaster Recovery"**
Coates' Canons post by Adam Lovelady
Available here: https://canons.sog.unc.edu/2024/10/adjusting-development-regulations-for-disaster-recovery

---

28. Mosquito Abatement Contract, https://www.ncdps.gov/our-organization/emergency -management/disaster-recovery/public-assistance/mosquito-abatement-contract (last visited May 13, 2026).

▶ **"Planning and Permitting Aspects of Helene Recovery Legislation"**
Coates' Canons post by Adam Lovelady
Available here: https://canons.sog.unc.edu/2024/10/planning-and-permitting-aspects-of-helene-recovery
-legislation/

▶ **"More Planning and Permitting Aspects of Helene Recovery Legislation"**
Coates' Canons post by Adam Lovelady
Available here: https://canons.sog.unc.edu/2025/01/more-planning-and-permitting-aspects-of-helene-recovery
-legislation/

▶ **"Historic Preservation and Community Resilience in North Carolina"**
Coates' Canons post by Adam Lovelady
Available here: https://canons.sog.unc.edu/2024/09/historic-preservation-and-community-resilience-in-north
-carolina/

▶ **"Temporary Housing and Zoning Amendments"**
Coates' Canons post by Adam Lovelady
Available here: https://canons.sog.unc.edu/2018/10/temporary-housing-and-zoning-amendments/

▶ **"Remote Zoning Hearings During Declared Emergencies"**
Coates' Canons post by Adam Lovelady
Available here: https://canons.sog.unc.edu/2020/05/remote-zoning-hearings-during-declared-emergencies/

Select Other Publications

▶ *Historic Resilience Primer: Resilient Adaptation Strategies for North Carolina's Historic Properties*
Available for download here: https://hrp.sog.unc.edu/wp-content/uploads/2023/10/HRP_Primer_Web_2023
-10-26.pdf

▶ *A Handbook for Historic Resilience Community Planning: Protecting North Carolina's History, Culture, and Economy from Natural Hazards*
Available for download here: https://hrp.sog.unc.edu/wp-content/uploads/2023/10/HRP_Handbook_Web_2023
-10-24.pdf

▶ *Resilience Design Standards: Model Standards for North Carolina's Historic Properties*
Available for download here: https://hrp.sog.unc.edu/wp-content/uploads/2023/10/HRP_DesignStandards
_Web_2023-10-26.pdf

▶ **Additional resources related to historic resilience and hazard mitigation**
Available for download here: https://hrp.sog.unc.edu/wp-content/uploads/2023/10/2023-10-04_RHP_Useful
_Resources.pdf

○○○ Other Miscellaneous Resource

Development Finance Initiative

The Development Finance Initiative (DFI) at the School of Government may be able to support local governments interested in development projects after an emergency, particularly those projects involving private investment.[29] More information about DFI's capabilities can be found at the DFI website, https://dfi.sog.unc.edu.[30]

---

29. *See* Development Finance Initiative, https://dfi.sog.unc.edu (last visited May 13, 2026).
30. *See id.*

School of Government Faculty

▶ **Adam Lovelady**
adamlovelady@sog.unc.edu

▶ **Jim Joyce**
jljoyce@sog.unc.edu

Employment

"First Stop" Resources

▶ Your local government human resources department

▶ Your county and/or municipal attorney

▶ Your county and/or municipal emergency manager

▶ Your local human resources, hiring, and employment policies and procedures

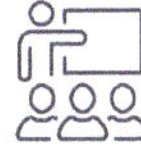

Select Trainings

FEMA Emergency Management Institute Independent Study Trainings

These trainings are free and self-paced.[31] Users may receive a certificate of completion after passing the final exam for the training.[32] Taking the exam may require setting up a Student ID with FEMA.[33] More information on FEMA Student IDs can be found on the FEMA website: https://cdp.dhs.gov/femasid.[34] Readers can also see the entire independent study course list on the FEMA website: https://training.fema.gov/is/crslist.aspx.[35]

▶ **IS-906: Workplace Security Awareness**
Page with links to course and exam located here: https://training.fema.gov/is/courseoverview.aspx?code=IS-906

▶ **IS-914: Surveillance Awareness: What You Can Do**
Page with links to course and exam located here: https://training.fema.gov/is/courseoverview.aspx?code=IS-914

▶ **IS-915: Protecting Critical Infrastructure Against Insider Threats**
Page with links to course and exam located here: https://training.fema.gov/is/courseoverview.aspx?code=IS-915

---

31. *See* Distance Learning, https://training.fema.gov/is/ (last visited May 13, 2026).

32. *See* Frequently Asked Questions (FAQs), https://training.fema.gov/is/isfaq.aspx (last visited May 13, 2026).

33. *See* Federal Emergency Management Agency Student Identification System, https://cdp.dhs.gov/femasid/#faq (last visited May 13, 2026) (expand the "Frequently Asked Questions" portion, which notes that "[a] FEMA SID [Student Identification] is required to register for and participate in any training provided by FEMA").

34. Federal Emergency Management Agency Student Identification System, https://cdp.dhs.gov/femasid (last visited May 13, 2026).

35. ISP Courses, https://training.fema.gov/is/crslist.aspx (last visited May 13, 2026).

Select Publications

▶ **Are You Prepared? Legal Issues Facing North Carolina Public Employers in Disasters and Other Emergencies**
Book by Diane Juffras
Available for purchase here: https://www.sog.unc.edu/publications/books/are-you-prepared-legal-issues-facing-north-carolina-public-employers-disasters-and-other-emergencies

▶ **"Hiring Retired Local Government Staff to Aid in Helene Response"**
Coates' Canons post by Kara Millonzi
Available here: https://canons.sog.unc.edu/2024/10/hiring-retired-local-government-staff-to-aid-in-helene-response/

▶ **"Liability Issues in Emergency Management for Local Governments"**
Coates' Canons post by Becca Fisher-Gabbard
Available here: https://canons.sog.unc.edu/2024/10/liability-issues-in-emergency-management-for-local-governments/

Select Potentially Relevant Law

▶ **G.S. 166A-19.60**
Immunity and liability provisions related to emergency management workers
Available here: https://www.ncleg.net/enactedlegislation/statutes/html/bysection/chapter_166a/gs_166a-19.60.html

School of Government Faculty

▶ **Diane Juffras**
juffras@sog.unc.edu

Finance and Tax

"First Stop" Resources

▶ Your local government's finance or budget officers/finance or budget department
▶ Your county and/or municipal attorney
▶ Your county and/or municipal emergency manager

Select Publications

▶ **"Budgeting for Disaster Recovery Cashflow Loans"**
Coates' Canons post by Kara Millonzi
Available here: https://canons.sog.unc.edu/2025/04/budgeting-for-disaster-recovery-cashflow-loans/

▶ **"Budgeting for FEMA Reimbursements, Preauditing Expenditures, Contracting Authority, and Managing Cash Flow During a Disaster"**
Coates' Canons post by Kara Millonzi
Available here: https://canons.sog.unc.edu/2024/10/budgeting-for-fema-reimbursements-preauditing
-expenditures-contracting-authority-and-managing-cash-flow-during-a-disaster/

▶ **"Local Government Soliciting and Receiving Donations During an Emergency"**
Coates' Canons post by Kara Millonzi
Available here: https://canons.sog.unc.edu/2024/10/local-government-soliciting-and-receiving-donations
-during-an-emergency/

▶ **"Financial Resiliency and Future Plans"**
Community and Economic Development in North Carolina and Beyond post by Carol Rosenfeld
Available here: https://ced.sog.unc.edu/2019/02/financial-resiliency-and-future-plans/

▶ **"Local Tax Issues Following a Natural Disaster"**
Coates' Canons post by Chris McLaughlin
Available here: https://canons.sog.unc.edu/2024/10/local-tax-issues-following-a-natural-disaster/

▶ **"North Carolina Assessors and Disaster Recovery"**
Death & Taxes post by Kirk Boone
Available here: https://deathandtaxes.sog.unc.edu/north-carolina-assessors-and-disaster-recovery/

○○○ Other Miscellaneous Resources

NC Finance Connect Office Hours

"Professor Kara Millonzi hosts weekly-ish office hours by Zoom on local government finance topic areas of interest."[36] See the NC Finance Connect website for information on upcoming office hour times and the Zoom link.[37]

Available here: https://ncfinanceconnect.com/office-hours/

State and Local Government Finance Division of the North Carolina Department of State Treasurer

The State and Local Government Finance Division of the North Carolina Department of State Treasurer webpage contains a link to the Local Government Commission staff blog and contact information.[38]

Available here: https://www.nctreasurer.gov/divisions/state-and-local-government-finance

---

36. OFFICE HOURS, https://ncfinanceconnect.com/office-hours/ (last visited May 13, 2026).

37. *Id.*

38. *See* STATE AND LOCAL GOVERNMENT FINANCE, https://www.nctreasurer.gov/divisions/state-and
-local-government-finance (last visited May 13, 2026).

School of Government Faculty

▶ **Kara Millonzi**
  • *Local government finance law*
  millonzi@sog.unc.edu

▶ **Bill Rivenbark**
  • *Local government financial management*
  rivenbark@sog.unc.edu

▶ **Greg Allison**
  • *Local government accounting and
     financial reporting*
  allison@sog.unc.edu

▶ **Chris McLaughlin**
  • *Local government tax law*
  mclaughlin@sog.unc.edu

▶ **Kirk Boone**
  • *Tax appraisal and assessment*
  boone@sog.unc.edu

Floodplain Management/National Flood Insurance Program (NFIP)

"First Stop" Resources

▶ Your local government's floodplain administrator
▶ Your county and/or municipal attorney
▶ Your county and/or municipal emergency manager
▶ Your local floodplain regulations

Select Trainings

NFIP101

This introductory floodplain management course is on-demand and offered through the Association of State Floodplain Managers (ASFPM).[39] Accessing the course requires an account with ASFPM.[40]

You can find more information here: https://www.floods.org/training-center/online -training/asfpm-on-demand-learning/nfip101/.

---

39. NFIP101, https://www.floods.org/training-center/online-training/asfpm-on-demand-learning /nfip101/ (last visited May 13, 2026).
40. *Id.*

FEMA Essentials of Floodplain Management Course

FEMA's Floodplain Management Division made "[t]his course," which "provides a broad overview of the NFIP and floodplain management."[41] It is an in-person offering that could be given as "a full day (8 hour) or half-day (4 hour) session."[42] FEMA notes that taking the "course does not adequately prepare participants to become a Floodplain Administrator."[43]

Those interested in requesting the course or learning more could contact FEMA's National Floodplain Management Training Team at fema-fpmtraining@fema.dhs.gov or contact the North Carolina State NFIP Coordinator.[44] The North Carolina State NFIP Coordinator is Steve Garrett, reachable at 919-825-2316 or Steve.Garrett@ncdps.gov.[45]

The FEMA website page with information on this course (and others) is here: https://www.fema.gov/floodplain-management/training/courses.

FEMA Emergency Management Institute Independent Study Trainings

These trainings are free and self-paced.[46] Users may receive a certificate of completion after passing the final exam for the training.[47] Taking the exam may require setting up a Student ID with FEMA.[48] More information on FEMA Student IDs can be found on the FEMA website: https://cdp.dhs.gov/femasid.[49] Readers can also see the entire independent study course list on the FEMA website: https://training.fema.gov/is/crslist.aspx.[50]

▶ **IS-273: How to Read a Flood Insurance Rate Map (FIRM)**
Page with links to course and exam located here: https://training.fema.gov/is/courseoverview.aspx?code=IS-273

▶ **IS-274: How to Use a Flood Insurance Study (FIS)**
Page with links to course and exam located here: https://training.fema.gov/is/courseoverview.aspx?code=IS-274

---

41. Floodplain Management Courses, https://www.fema.gov/floodplain-management/training/courses (last visited May 13, 2026).

42. *Id.*

43. *Id.*

44. *See id.* (clicking the "FEMA National FPM Training Team" hyperlink shows the listed email address).

45. State NFIP Coordinators (SCs), https://www.floods.org/membership-communities/connect/state-floodplain-managers-scs/ (last visited May 13, 2026) (navigate to and click on the "NC" portion of the page to find the contact information).

46. *See* Distance Learning, https://training.fema.gov/is/ (last visited May 13, 2026).

47. *See* Frequently Asked Questions (FAQs), https://training.fema.gov/is/isfaq.aspx (last visited May 13, 2026).

48. *See* Federal Emergency Management Agency Student Identification System, https://cdp.dhs.gov/femasid/#faq (last visited May 13, 2026) (expand the "Frequently Asked Questions" portion, which notes that "[a] FEMA SID [Student Identification] is required to register for and participate in any training provided by FEMA").

49. Federal Emergency Management Agency Student Identification System, https://cdp.dhs.gov/femasid (last visited May 13, 2026).

50. ISP Courses, https://training.fema.gov/is/crslist.aspx (last visited May 13, 2026).

FEMA Floodplain Management Division Recorded Webinars

FEMA's Floodplain Management division has recorded floodplain management webinars accessible online.[51] They appear aimed at floodplain administrators or people with higher familiarity with floodplain management.[52] The webinars available are:

- *NFIP Compliance Audit Program: Overview Webinar*
- *Elevation Certificate Webinar*
- *Floodproofing Webinar*
- *How to Perform a No-Rise Analysis Under 2D Conditions*[53]

You can access the webinars here: https://www.fema.gov/floodplain-management/training/webinars.

Select Publications

▶ **Frequently Asked Questions About Local Floodplain Regulations in North Carolina**
Publication by Adam Lovelady and Steve Garrett
Available here: https://www.sog.unc.edu/sites/default/files/Floodplain%20FAQs%2011_12_2024.pdf

▶ **North Carolina Floodplain Management: 2017 Quick Guide**
Publication from the North Carolina Division of Emergency Management
Available here: https://flood.nc.gov/NCFLOOD_BUCKET/FAQS/QuickGuideTopic/NCQuickGuide2017.pdf

▶ **CRS Discount Frequently Asked Questions**
Fact sheet by FEMA
Available here: https://www.fema.gov/sites/default/files/documents/fema-nfip-community-rating-system-discount-faq-09-2024.pdf

▶ **"Act Locally, Save Federally: The National Flood Insurance CRS Program"**
Community and Economic Development in North Carolina and Beyond post by Jeffrey Hughes
Available here: https://ced.sog.unc.edu/2018/04/act-locally-save-federally-the-national-flood-insurance-crs-program/

▶ **"Local Government Strategies for Mitigating the Risks of Flooding"**
Community and Economic Development in North Carolina and Beyond post by Mary Tiger
Available here: https://ced.sog.unc.edu/2015/02/local-government-strategies-for-mitigating-the-risks-of-flooding/

---

51. Floodplain Management Webinars, https://www.fema.gov/floodplain-management/training/webinars (last visited May 13, 2026).

52. *See id.*

53. *Id.*

Select Potentially Relevant Laws

▶ **G.S. 143, Article 21, Part 6, Floodway Regulation (G.S. 143-215.51 through G.S. 143-215.61)**

Local government authority to engage in floodplain management; requirements for local government floodplain management ordinances; and other related topics
Available here: https://www.ncleg.gov/EnactedLegislation/Statutes/HTML/ByArticle/Chapter_143/Article_21.html

▶ **Various federal provisions**

FEMA provides an overview of federal laws related to floodplain management and the National Flood Insurance Program on their website.[54]
Available here: https://www.fema.gov/flood-insurance/rules-legislation/laws

Other Miscellaneous Resources

FEMA Floodplain Management Videos

FEMA offers several videos related to floodplain management and NFIP topics.[55] The videos are entitled:

- *Higher Standards: The Value of Floodplain Management*
- *Floodplain Management: Higher Standards*
- *Floodplain Management: Freeboard*
- *Higher Standards: Increased Cost of Compliance*
- *Disaster Recovery Reform Act 1206*[56]

The videos are available here: https://www.fema.gov/floodplain-management/training/videos.

FEMA "Know Your Risk" Page for State, Local, Tribal, and Territorial Governments

FEMA has a page that links to various additional floodplain-management-related resources related to local governments, including resources related to hurricanes, dams, and general flood hazard mitigation.[57] That page is located here: https://www.fema.gov/flood-maps/know-your-risk/government. Listing all of the resources that stem from this page would require significant space. Users can use this page as a starting point, navigate themselves, and locate the resources that may be most helpful.

---

54. Laws and Regulations, https://www.fema.gov/flood-insurance/rules-legislation/laws (last visited May 13, 2026).

55. Floodplain Management Videos, https://www.fema.gov/floodplain-management/training/videos (last visited May 13, 2026).

56. *Id.*

57. Know Your Risk: State, Local, Tribal or Territorial Governments, https://www.fema.gov/flood-maps/know-your-risk/government (last visited May 13, 2026).

FEMA Managing Floodplains for Local Elected Officials and Executives Resource

This item is a set of training materials that local government staff can use to train other local government staff and elected officials.[58] It is designed as teaching materials "to help floodplain administrators explain floodplain management to [their] community's senior leadership."[59]

The materials are located here: https://www.fema.gov/floodplain-management/training /courses/local-elected-executive.

State, Federal, Nonprofit, or Professional Organization Contacts

NFIP

Users may contact the individuals below from the North Carolina Department of Public Safety's Division of Emergency Management (NCEM) for questions related to the National Flood Insurance Program.[60] The "Western," "Central," or "Eastern" planners may be most appropriate as contacts for local governments in specific regions of North Carolina.[61]

▶ **Steve Garrett, CFM**
State NFIP Coordinator
919-825-2316
Steve.Garrett@ncdps.gov

▶ **Jintao Wen, PhD, P.E.**
NFIP Engineer
919-825-2317
Jintao.Wen@ncdps.gov

▶ **Terry Foxx, CFM**
Western NFIP Planner
828-228-8526
Terry.Foxx@ncdps.gov

▶ **Matthew Stillwagon**
Central NFIP Planner
919-825-2289
Matthew.Stillwagon@ncdps.gov

▶ **Eryn Futral, AICP, CFM, CZO**
Eastern NFIP Planner
919-819-1734
Eryn.Futral@ncdps.gov

School of Government Faculty

▶ **Adam Lovelady**
adamlovelady@sog.unc.edu

▶ **Taylor Morris**
morris@sog.unc.edu

---

58. Managing Floodplains for Local, Elected Officials and Executives, https://www.fema .gov/floodplain-management/training/courses/local-elected-executive (last visited May 13, 2026).

59. *Id.*

60. *See* email and attachment from Steve Garrett to Taylor Morris (May 30, 2025, 07:09 AM EDT) (on file with author).

61. *Cf. id.* (showing a map dividing North Carolina into three regions).

General/Miscellaneous Emergency Management

"First Stop" Resources

▶ Your municipal and/or county emergency manager

▶ Your municipal and/or county attorney

Select Trainings

NC Training Exercise Response Management System (NC TERMS) Trainings

Users can create an NC TERMS account and sign up for a variety of in-person or online trainings related to emergency management.[62]

The home page for NC TERMS is located here: https://terms.ncem.gov/TRS/. Interested users may explore what training options are available.

FEMA Trainings

FEMA Emergency Management Institute Independent Study Trainings

These trainings are free and self-paced.[63] Users may receive a certificate of completion after passing the final exam for the training.[64] Taking the exam may require setting up a Student ID with FEMA.[65] More information on FEMA Student IDs can be found on the FEMA website: https://cdp.dhs.gov/femasid.[66] Readers can also see the entire independent study course list on the FEMA website: https://training.fema.gov/is/crslist.aspx.[67]

▶ **IS-100.C: Introduction to the Incident Command System, ICS 100***

Page with links to course and exam located here: https://training.fema.gov/is/courseoverview.aspx?code=IS-100.c

▶ **IS-200.C: Basic Incident Command System for Initial Response, ICS-200***

Page with links to course and exam located here: https://training.fema.gov/is/courseoverview.aspx?code=IS-200.c

▶ **IS-230.E: Fundamentals of Emergency Management**

Page with links to course and exam located here: https://training.fema.gov/is/courseoverview.aspx?code=IS-230.e

---

62. *Cf.* North Carolina TERMS, https://terms.ncem.gov/TRS/ (last visited May 13, 2026) (showing an account creation option); Calendar, https://terms.ncem.gov/TRS/courseSearch.do (last visited May 13, 2026) (listing training opportunities).

63. *See* Distance Learning, https://training.fema.gov/is/ (last visited May 13, 2026).

64. *See* Frequently Asked Questions (FAQs), https://training.fema.gov/is/isfaq.aspx (last visited May 13, 2026).

65. *See* Federal Emergency Management Agency Student Identification System, https://cdp.dhs.gov/femasid/#faq (last visited May 13, 2026) (expand the "Frequently Asked Questions" portion, which notes that "[a] FEMA SID [Student Identification] is required to register for and participate in any training provided by FEMA").

66. Federal Emergency Management Agency Student Identification System, https://cdp.dhs.gov/femasid/ (last visited May 13, 2026).

67. ISP Courses, https://training.fema.gov/is/crslist.aspx (last visited May 13, 2026).

▶ **IS-700.B: An Introduction to the National Incident Management System***

Page with links to course and exam located here: https://training.fema.gov/is/courseoverview.aspx?code=IS-700.b

▶ **IS-800.D: National Response Framework, An Introduction***

Page with link to study materials and exam is located on the FEMA website: https://training.fema.gov/is/courseoverview.aspx?code=IS-800.d. Per the Emergency Management Institute website, the actual course appears not to be accessible.[68] However, the site provides a link to study materials that could be used to take the course's exam online and receive the course's completion certificate after passage.[69]

* These courses may be prerequisites or recommended foundations for other independent study trainings.[70]

FEMA Just-in-Time Recovery Management Training

This free, in-person, interactive training opportunity aims to help local governments with recovery after an event occurs. The training takes place over three non-consecutive days at different points in the process of recovery: (1) one day around two months after a disaster declaration, (2) one day around three to five months after a disaster declaration, and (3) a final day around six months or more after a disaster declaration. Each training day is intended to provide information connected to the part of the recovery process when the training is occurring and adds to learning from previous training. The local government receiving the training may choose where the training occurs. FEMA notes that this training is introductory and is not a detailed, complete course on managing disaster recovery. FEMA also seems to intend to keep classes for this training small.[71]

You may contact Veanda Simmons (veanda.simmons@fema.dhs.gov) or CA-RSF@fema.dhs.gov.[72]

---

68. *See* IS-800.D: National Response Framework, An Introduction, https://training.fema.gov/is/courseoverview.aspx?code=IS-800.d (last visited May 13, 2026).

69. *See id.*

70. *See, e.g.*, IS-706: NIMS Intrastate Mutual Aid—An Introduction, https://training.fema.gov/is/courseoverview.aspx?code=IS-706 (last visited May 13, 2026) (listing IS-700 as a prerequisite); IS-822: Fundamentals of Management and Support Coordination of Federal Disaster Operations, https://training.fema.gov/is/courseoverview.aspx?code=IS-822 (last visited May 13, 2026) (listing IS-100.c, IS-200.c, IS-700.b, and IS-800.d as prerequisites); IS-703.B: National Incident Management System Resource Management, https://training.fema.gov/is/courseoverview.aspx?code=IS-703.b (last visited May 13, 2026) (listing "IS 0700" as a recommended prior course); IS-802.A: Emergency Support Function (ESF) #2—Communications, https://training.fema.gov/is/courseoverview.aspx?code=IS-802.a (last visited May 13, 2026) (listing "IS0100.c," "IS0700.b," and "IS0800.d" as recommended prior courses).

71. *See* email and attachment from John Griego to Taylor Morris (June 23, 2025, 03:42 PM EDT) (on file with author).

72. *See id.*

Select Publications

Select FEMA Publications

▶ *Developing and Maintaining Emergency Operations Plans*

▶ *Local Elected and Appointed Officials Guide: Roles and Resources in Emergency Management*
   Available here: https://www.fema.gov/sites/default/files/documents/fema_npd_local-elected-officials-guide_2025.pdf

▶ *FEMA Preliminary Damage Assessment Guide*
   Available here: https://www.fema.gov/sites/default/files/documents/fema_rd_pda-guide_07012025.pdf

▶ *PDA Pocket Guide*
   Available here: https://www.fema.gov/sites/default/files/documents/fema_rd_pda-pocket-guide_07012025.pdf

▶ *Preliminary Damage Assessment Guide: Summary of Changes*
   Available here: https://www.fema.gov/sites/default/files/documents/fema_rd_pda-guide-summary-of-changes_07012025.pdf

▶ *National Incident Management System, Third Edition*
   Available here: https://www.fema.gov/sites/default/files/2020-07/fema_nims_doctrine-2017.pdf

▶ *National Incident Management System Training Program*
   Available here: https://www.fema.gov/sites/default/files/documents/fema_nims-training-program-2020.pdf

▶ *National Incident Management System Basic Guidance for Public Information Officers*
   Available here: https://www.fema.gov/sites/default/files/documents/fema_nims-basic-guidance-public-information-officers_12-2020.pdf

Select School of Government Publications

▶ *"Misinformation and Threats on Social Media in the Wake of Hurricane Helene: How Local Governments Can Respond"*
   Coates' Canons post by Kristi Nickodem
   Available here: https://canons.sog.unc.edu/2024/10/misinformation-and-threats-on-social-media-in-the-wake-of-hurricane-helene-how-local-governments-can-respond/

▶ **"Natural Hazard Mitigation Saves Lives, Money, and Property"**
   Community and Economic Development in North Carolina and Beyond post by Brian Dabson
   Available here: https://ced.sog.unc.edu/2018/03/natural-hazard-mitigation-saves-lives-money-and-property/

▶ **"Strengthening Resilience in North Carolina's Communities"**
   Community and Economic Development in North Carolina and Beyond post by Brian Dabson
   Available here: https://ced.sog.unc.edu/2016/12/strengthening-resilience-in-north-carolinas-communities/

▶ **"Community Resilience Has Many Faces…Part 1"**
   Community and Economic Development in North Carolina and Beyond post by Brian Dabson
   Available here: https://ced.sog.unc.edu/2017/01/community-resilience-has-many-faces-part-1/

▶ **"Community Resilience Has Many Faces…Part 2"**

Community and Economic Development in North Carolina and Beyond post by Brian Dabson

Available here: https://ced.sog.unc.edu/2017/03/07/community-resilience-has-many-facespart-2/

▶ **"Community Resilience: Some Practical Questions"**

Community and Economic Development in North Carolina and Beyond post by Brian Dabson

Available here: https://ced.sog.unc.edu/2017/06/community-resilience-some-practical-questions/

Select Other Publication

▶ ***North Carolina State Emergency Response Team, Hurricane Helene After Action Review: Final Report***

Report by Erin Sutton, Ryan Arzamarski, and the McChrystal Group, commissioned by the North Carolina Department of Public Safety's Division of Emergency Management (NCEM)

Available here: https://www.ncdps.gov/division/emergency-management/ts-helene-after-action-review/open

Select Potentially Relevant Laws

▶ **44 C.F.R. Chapter 1 (Parts 1–399)**

General FEMA regulations

Available here: https://www.ecfr.gov/current/title-44/chapter-I

▶ **G.S. 166A-19.3**

Definitions of terms as used in the North Carolina Emergency Management Act

Available here: https://www.ncleg.gov/EnactedLegislation/Statutes/HTML/BySection/Chapter_166A/GS_166A-19.3.html

▶ **G.S. 166A-19.15**

Describes certain county emergency management responsibility and various local government emergency management powers

Available here: https://www.ncleg.gov/EnactedLegislation/Statutes/HTML/BySection/Chapter_166A/GS_166A-19.15.html

▶ **G.S. 166A-19.22**

State of emergency declarations for municipalities and counties

Available here: https://www.ncleg.gov/EnactedLegislation/Statutes/HTML/BySection/Chapter_166A/GS_166A-19.22.html

▶ **G.S. 166A-19.30(c)**

Certain powers of the governor over local governments during states of emergency declared by the governor or the legislature

Available here: https://www.ncleg.gov/EnactedLegislation/Statutes/HTML/BySection/Chapter_166A/GS_166A-19.30.html

▶ **G.S. 166A-19.31**

Local government powers to pass ordinances authorizing emergency prohibitions and restrictions and impose prohibitions or restrictions during locally declared states of emergency

Available here: https://www.ncleg.gov/EnactedLegislation/Statutes/HTML/BySection/Chapter_166A/GS_166A-19.31.html

○○○ Other Miscellaneous Resources

FEMA YouTube Channel

General FEMA channel with educational videos on a variety of FEMA-related topics.[73] The channel is available here: https://www.youtube.com/@FEMA.

FEMA Damage Assessment Resources

FEMA offers links to resources like damage assessment templates and a checklist (in English and Spanish) related to initial damage assessments.[74] The resources are available here: https://www.fema.gov/disaster/how-declared/preliminary-damage-assessments.

North Carolina Emergency Management Weather Update Distribution List

The North Carolina Department of Public Safety's Division of Emergency Management (NCEM) has a weather update distribution list that provides daily hazardous weather information.[75] To subscribe to that list, local government staff may email Diana.Thomas@ncdps.gov or Michael.Duquette@ncdps.gov.[76]

National Weather Service

The National Weather Service's website contains links to a wide variety of resources, from information on current severe weather threats, brochures, educational content, general information on various types of weather hazards, and more.[77] For brevity, all of these resources are not included here. Interested users may explore these resources by going here: https://www.weather.gov/ and navigating.

NC Local Government Disaster Recovery Portal

The NC Local Government Disaster Recovery Portal is a website that provides information on recovery-related resources for North Carolina local governments, especially on recovery funding.[78] Users may be able to find recovery funding opportunities; learn about relevant funding deadlines; identify trainings and office hours to help learn more; and find contact information for people or entities that might be able to offer help.[79] The portal is available here: https://ncrecoveryportal.com.

---

73. *See* FEMA, https://www.youtube.com/@FEMA (last visited May 13, 2026).

74. Preliminary Damage Assessments, https://www.fema.gov/disaster/how-declared/preliminary -damage-assessments (last visited May 13, 2026).

75. *See* email from Diana Thomas to Taylor Morris (June 20, 2025, 07:59 AM EDT) (on file with author).

76. *See id.*

77. *See* National Forecast Maps, https://www.weather.gov/forecastmaps/ (last visited May 13, 2026); NWS and Partners Publications and Brochures, https://www.weather.gov/owlie/publication _brochures (last visited May 13, 2026); Weather Safety for All Hazards, https://www.weather.gov /safety/ (last visited May 13, 2026); NWS Education, https://www.weather.gov/education/ (last visited May 13, 2026); NWS Newsletters, Service Assessments and Major Reports, https://www.weather .gov/publications/ (last visited May 13, 2026).

78. NC Local Government Disaster Recovery Portal, https://ncrecoveryportal.com/ (last visited May 13, 2026).

79. *Id.*

School of Government Listservs

The School of Government offers a wide variety of email listservs to which users may be able to subscribe.[80] The listservs generally give users the ability to reach out to and receive messages from other subscribers via the listserv. They cover a wide variety of topics, including emergency management.[81] However, many other listservs exist for specialty areas that may be more appropriate for certain emergency-management-related content.[82] For instance, listservs exist for grants management or permitting that might be better places to direct grants or permitting content.[83] Different listservs have different features and criteria for joining.[84] Interested users can survey the listserv options and learn about subscribing on the School of Government website, https://www.sog.unc.edu/resources/microsites/listserv/listserv-list.[85]

North Carolina Resilience Exchange Resources

The North Carolina Resilience Exchange, a state resource, has a variety of resources that may be of use to North Carolina local governments interested in emergency resiliency.[86] The main page of their general website is here: https://www.resilienceexchange.nc.gov/.

North Carolina Resilience Exchange Ordinance Resources

The North Carolina Resilience Exchange has a page that contains sample local government ordinances related to resiliency.[87] That page is located here: https://www.resilienceexchange.nc.gov/find-resources/find-resources-ordinance-resources-north-carolina.

North Carolina Resilience Exchange State and Local Plan Resources

The North Carolina Resilience Exchange has a page that gives examples of plans focused on resiliency at the state and local government level in North Carolina.[88] That page is located here: https://www.resilienceexchange.nc.gov/find-resources/find-resources-state-and-local-plans.

---

80. *See* LISTSERVS, https://www.sog.unc.edu/resources/microsites/listserv/listserv-list (last visited May 13, 2026).

81. *Id.*

82. *Id.*

83. *Id.*

84. *Id.*

85. *Id.*

86. *See* FIND RESOURCES: ORDINANCE RESOURCES FOR NORTH CAROLINA, https://www.resilienceexchange.nc.gov/find-resources/find-resources-ordinance-resources-north-carolina (last visited May 13, 2026); FIND RESOURCES: STATE AND LOCAL PLANS, https://www.resilienceexchange.nc.gov/find-resources/find-resources-state-and-local-plans (last visited May 13, 2026); REPORTS AND TOOLS, https://www.resilienceexchange.nc.gov/find-resources/tools (last visited May 13, 2026).

87. FIND RESOURCES: ORDINANCE RESOURCES FOR NORTH CAROLINA, https://www.resilienceexchange.nc.gov/find-resources/find-resources-ordinance-resources-north-carolina (last visited May 13, 2026).

88. FIND RESOURCES: STATE AND LOCAL PLANS, https://www.resilienceexchange.nc.gov/find-resources/find-resources-state-and-local-plans (last visited May 13, 2026).

North Carolina Resilience Exchange Reports and Tools Page
The North Carolina Resilience Exchange has a page that allows its users to navigate to a wide variety of resilience-related resources, including reports, mapping tools, and websites.[89] It contains a search bar; a way to filter by type of resource; and a way to filter to find resources related to different "Action Types," "Assets," or "Hazards."[90] For brevity, all of these resources are not listed here. Users can visit the page and navigate on their own to see what resources might help them. That page is located here: https://www.resilienceexchange.nc.gov /find-resources/tools.

State, Federal, Nonprofit, or Professional Organization Contacts

Select General North Carolina Department of Public Safety Division of Emergency Management (NCEM) Contacts

General Contacts

▶ **NCEM General Mailing Address**
  4236 Mail Service Center
  Raleigh, NC 27699-4236

▶ **Main Switchboard Phone Number**
  919-825-2500

▶ **24-Hour Watch Center Phone Number**
  919-733-3300

▶ **Director's Fax**
  919-825-2685

▶ **Western Branch Office Phone Number**
  828-466-5555

▶ **Central Branch Office Phone Number**
  336-329-1302

▶ **Eastern Branch Office Phone Number**
  252-520-4923[91]

Emergency Planning Contact
Local governments with questions about developing emergency-related plans may contact Kate Dunlap at Kate.Dunlap@ncdps.gov or 919-815-8835.[92]

---

89. Reports and Tools, https://www.resilienceexchange.nc.gov/find-resources/tools (last visited May 13, 2026).

90. *Id.*

91. Contact NC Emergency Management, https://www.ncdps.gov/our-organization/emergency -management/contact-nc-emergency-management (last visited May 13, 2026) (listing this contact information).

92. *See* email from Kate Dunlap to Taylor Morris (Oct. 13, 2025, 08:24 AM EDT) (on file with author).

FEMA Region 4 Contacts

FEMA's Region 4 includes North Carolina and several other states, along with several Tribal Nations.[93] The general phone number for FEMA's Region 4 is 770-220-5200, and the general email address is FEMA-R4-Info@fema.dhs.gov.[94]

FEMA Preliminary Damage Assessment Contact

Users may contact FEMA-Recovery-PDA@fema.dhs.gov for questions to FEMA about preliminary damage assessments.[95]

North Carolina League of Municipalities (NCLM) Helene Resources

NCLM has a page containing a variety of Helene-related resources and contact information, available here: https://www.nclm.org/insurance-risk-management/hurricane-helene.[96]

North Carolina Association of County Commissioners (NCACC) Helene Resources

NCACC has a page containing a variety of Helene-related resources and contact information, available here: https://www.ncacc.org/services-for-counties/hurricane-helene-resources/.[97]

School of Government Faculty

▶ **Taylor Morris**
- *General emergency management law*
- *Code enforcement law*
morris@sog.unc.edu

▶ **Kara Millonzi**
- *General county law*
- *Local government finance law*
- *Local government utilities*
millonzi@sog.unc.edu

▶ **Becca Fisher-Gabbard**
- *General municipal law*
- *Local government legal authority*
- *Local government liability and immunity*
rfisher@sog.unc.edu

▶ **Kristina Wilson**
- *General municipal law*
- *Public meetings/public records/open government*
- *Local government board procedures*
wilson@sog.unc.edu

▶ **Kim Nelson**
- *Local government leadership and management*
knelson@sog.unc.edu

▶ **Teshanee Williams**
- *Local government and nonprofit relationships*
- *Community engagement*
twilliams@sog.unc.edu

---

93. Region 4, https://www.fema.gov/about/regions/region-4 (last visited May 13, 2026).

94. *Id.*

95. Preliminary Damage Assessment (PDA) Overview, https://www.youtube.com/watch?v=O_4_TGRf5U8 (last visited May 13, 2026) (containing video listing email for contacting FEMA about preliminary damage assessments).

96. Hurricane Helene, https://www.nclm.org/insurance-risk-management/hurricane-helene (last visited May 13, 2026).

97. Hurricane Helene Resources, https://www.ncacc.org/services-for-counties/hurricane-helene-resources/ (last visited May 13, 2026).

If none of these faculty members works in the area where you need assistance, or if you are interested in a more detailed overview of faculty areas of expertise throughout the School of Government, you may use the Faculty Fields of Expertise list: https://www.sog.unc.edu /sites/default/files/FINAL20250157%20FacultyExpertise_Jan2026_4.pdf.[98] Users can also find faculty by navigating to the School of Government's website, then going to About, then Faculty & Staff.[99] Readers can also access the Faculty & Staff page on the School of Government website directly at https://www.sog.unc.edu/about/faculty-and-staff/.[100] Since this expertise list may be updated from time to time, the specific list linked above may become outdated. Visiting the School of Government's website may help users find a more updated list.

Grants

"First Stop" Resources

▶ Your local government's contracting/procurement/purchasing/finance department
▶ Your local government's grants manager
▶ Your county and/or municipal attorney
▶ Your county and/or municipal emergency manager

Select Trainings

FEMA Trainings

FEMA Emergency Management Institute Independent Study Trainings

These trainings are free and self-paced.[101] Users may receive a certificate of completion after passing the final exam for the training.[102] Taking the exam may require setting up a Student ID with FEMA.[103] More information on FEMA Student IDs can be found on the

---

98. *See* Faculty Fields of Expertise, January 2026, https://www.sog.unc.edu/sites/default/files /FINAL20250157%20FacultyExpertise_Jan2026_4.pdf (last visited May 13, 2026).

99. *See* Faculty and Staff, https://www.sog.unc.edu/about/faculty-and-staff/ (last visited May 13, 2026).

100. *See id.*

101. *See* Distance Learning, https://training.fema.gov/is/ (last visited May 13, 2026).

102. *See* Frequently Asked Questions (FAQs), https://training.fema.gov/is/isfaq.aspx (last visited May 13, 2026).

103. *See* Federal Emergency Management Agency Student Identification System, https://cdp.dhs.gov/femasid/#faq (last visited May 13, 2026) (expand the "Frequently Asked Questions" portion, which notes that "[a] FEMA SID [Student Identification] is required to register for and participate in any training provided by FEMA").

FEMA website: https://cdp.dhs.gov/femasid.[104] Readers can also see the entire independent study course list on the FEMA website: https://training.fema.gov/is/crslist.aspx.[105]

▶ **IS-1000: Public Assistance Program and Eligibility**
Page with links to course and exam located here: https://training.fema.gov/is/courseoverview.aspx?code=IS-1000

▶ **IS-1002: FEMA Grants Portal—Transparency at Every Step**
Page with links to course and exam located here: https://training.fema.gov/is/courseoverview.aspx?code=IS-1002

▶ **IS-1006: Documenting Disaster Damage and Developing Project Files**
Page with links to course and exam located here: https://training.fema.gov/is/courseoverview.aspx?code=IS-1006

▶ **IS-1007: Detailed Damage Description and Dimensions**
Page with links to course and exam located here: https://training.fema.gov/is/courseoverview.aspx?code=IS-1007

▶ **IS-1008: Scope of Work Development (Scoping and Costing)**
Page with links to course and exam located here: https://training.fema.gov/is/courseoverview.aspx?code=IS-1008

▶ **IS-1009: Conditions of the Public Assistance Grant**
Page with links to course and exam located here: https://training.fema.gov/is/courseoverview.aspx?code=IS-1009

▶ **IS-1011: Roads and Culverts**
Page with links to course and exam located here: https://training.fema.gov/is/courseoverview.aspx?code=IS-1011

▶ **IS-1014: Integrating 406 Mitigation Considerations into Your Public Assistance Grant**
Page with links to course and exam located here: https://training.fema.gov/is/courseoverview.aspx?code=IS-1014

▶ **IS-1015: Insurance Considerations, Compliance, and Requirements**
Page with links to course and exam located here: https://training.fema.gov/is/courseoverview.aspx?code=IS-1015

▶ **IS-1017: Scope Change Requests, Time Extensions, Improved/Alternate Project Requests**
Page with links to course and exam located here: https://training.fema.gov/is/courseoverview.aspx?code=IS-1017

▶ **IS-1021: Bridge Damage Considerations**
Page with links to course and exam located here: https://training.fema.gov/is/courseoverview.aspx?code=IS-1021

▶ **IS-1023: Electrical Systems Considerations**
Page with links to course and exam located here: https://training.fema.gov/is/courseoverview.aspx?code=IS-1023

Other FEMA Grants Training

▶ **Fundamentals of Grants Management Course**
This course has been scheduled with in-person and virtual options, though the in-person option appears to be at a specific location.[106] In other words, the course does not appear to be offered on-site for local governments.

More information about the course is on the FEMA website: https://www.fema.gov/grants/tools/technical-assistance. To learn more, you may also email: FEMA-GPD-Training@fema.dhs.gov.[107]

---

104. FEDERAL EMERGENCY MANAGEMENT AGENCY STUDENT IDENTIFICATION SYSTEM, https://cdp.dhs.gov/femasid (last visited May 13, 2026).

105. ISP COURSES, https://training.fema.gov/is/crslist.aspx (last visited May 13, 2026).

106. *See* FUNDAMENTALS OF GRANTS MANAGEMENT COURSE SCHEDULE (FISCAL YEAR 2026), https://www.fema.gov/sites/default/files/documents/fema_gmta-fy26-ek0705-course-schedule.pdf (last visited May 13, 2026) (listing in-person option in Maryland).

107. *See id.* (listing this email address).

Select Publications

▶ **Public Assistance Program and Policy Guide**
FEMA guide on the use of FEMA's Public Assistance program
Available here: https://www.fema.gov/sites/default/files/documents/fema_pa_pappg-v5.0_012025.pdf

▶ **"FEMA Emergency Work (Categories A and B)"**
Coates' Canons post by Rebecca Badgett
Available here: https://canons.sog.unc.edu/2024/10/fema-emergency-work-categories-a-and-b/

▶ **"Allocating the CDBG-Disaster Recovery Funds: Local Government and Citizen Participation Encouraged"**
Coates' Canons post by Rebecca Badgett
Available here: https://canons.sog.unc.edu/2025/02/allocating-the-cdbg-disaster-recovery-funds-local
-government-and-citizen-participation-encouraged/

▶ **"Overview of the 2024 Updates to the Federal Uniform Guidance"**
Coates' Canons post by Rebecca Badgett
Available here: https://canons.sog.unc.edu/2024/09/overview-of-the-2024-updates-to-the-federal-uniform
-guidance/

▶ **"Legal Limits on Local Government Authority to Accept State and Federal Grants and Loans"**
Coates' Canons post by Kara Millonzi
Available here: https://canons.sog.unc.edu/2025/06/legal-limits-on-local-government-authority-to-accept-state
-and-federal-grants-and-loans/

Select Potentially Relevant Laws

North Carolina Local Government Authority Related to Grants

▶ **G.S. 160A-17.1**
General municipal authority related to accepting or contracting for federal or state grants
Available here: http://ncleg.gov/enactedlegislation/statutes/html/bysection/chapter_160a/gs_160a-17.1.html

▶ **G.S. 153A-14**
General county authority related to contracting for and using grants
Available here: https://www.ncleg.gov/EnactedLegislation/Statutes/HTML/BySection/Chapter_153A/GS_153A-14.html

Procurement with Federal Grants in General

▶ **2 C.F.R. 200.317–27**
General federal procurement regulations
Available here: https://www.ecfr.gov/current/title-2/subtitle-A/chapter-II/part-200/subpart-D/subject-group
-ECFR45ddd4419ad436d

Community Development Block Grant Disaster Relief (CDBG-DR)

▶ **24 C.F.R. Part 570**
General federal regulations related to Community Development Block Grants
Available here: https://www.ecfr.gov/current/title-24/subtitle-B/chapter-V/subchapter-C/part-570

▶ ***Community Development Block Grant Disaster Recovery Universal Notice: Waivers and Alternative Requirements* ("Universal Notice" or UN)**
Explains requirements, procedures, and other information specifically related to the Community Development Block Grant Disaster Recovery program.[108]
Available here: https://www.hud.gov/sites/default/files/CPD/documents/Universal-Notice-04032025.pdf

FEMA Disaster Assistance

▶ **44 C.F.R. Part 206**
General federal regulations related to FEMA disaster assistance
Available here: https://www.ecfr.gov/current/title-44/chapter-I/subchapter-D/part-206

○○○ # Other Miscellaneous Resources

FEMA Public Assistance YouTube Channel
This channel provides videos related to FEMA Public Assistance.[109] Available here: https://www.youtube.com/channel/UCIJp91Ds2IaVlR1t8uXcEKg/videos

HUD Exchange YouTube Channel
The channel's full set of videos is available on YouTube: https://www.youtube.com /@HUDexchange. This YouTube channel contains two playlists that may be especially helpful for CDBG-DR grant issues:

- The "2024 CDBG-DR Problem Solving Clinic" playlist, available here: https://www.youtube.com/playlist?list=PLS7Yr7j8XXlZVPUHzyGkxDrDPitIllR8P.[110]
- The "CDBG-DR and CDBG-MIT Grantee-Led Sessions" playlist, available here: https://www.youtube.com/playlist?list=PLS7Yr7j8XXlZbQPEBxRiHzfa4dH5Jxdfm.[111]

HUD Exchange CDBG-DR Page
This page connects to various resources related to CDBG-DR grants, including guidance publications; information on relevant laws and regulations; and information on potential trainings.[112] For brevity, the index has not catalogued all of these potential resources throughout the Grants section. Users can click through this page and the pages connected to it and explore potential resources as appropriate for them. The page is available here: https://www.hudexchange.info/programs/cdbg-dr/.

---

108. Universal Notice Covered Grantees, https://www.hud.gov/stat/cpd/universal-notice-grantees (last visited May 13, 2026).

109. *See* FEMA Public Assistance, https://www.youtube.com/channel/UCIJp91Ds2IaVlR1t8uXcEKg /videos (last visited May 13, 2026).

110. *See* 2024 CDBG-DR Problem Solving Clinic, https://www.youtube.com/playlist?list =PLS7Yr7j8XXlZVPUHzyGkxDrDPitIllR8P (last visited May 13, 2026).

111. *See* CDBG-DR and CDBG-MIT Grantee-Led Sessions, https://www.youtube.com/playlist?list =PLS7Yr7j8XXlZbQPEBxRiHzfa4dH5Jxdfm (last visited May 13, 2026).

112. *See* CDBG Disaster Recovery Funds, https://www.hudexchange.info/programs/cdbg-dr/ (last visited May 13, 2026).

State, Federal, Nonprofit, or Professional Organization Contacts

Western NC Recovery Grants Program from North Carolina Department of Environmental Quality (DEQ)

DEQ may be able to offer assistance with grants to communities in Western North Carolina.[113] Those interested can visit the Western NC Recovery Grants Program site or contact Katie Hunt at Katie.Hunt@deq.nc.gov.[114]

State CDBG-DR Support

Local governments with questions about the Community Development Block Grant Disaster Relief grant may contact any of the following people at the North Carolina Department of Commerce:

▶ **Maggie Battaglin**
maggie.battaglin@commerce.nc.gov

▶ **Ayanna Wallace**
ayanna.wallace@commerce.nc.gov

▶ **Emily Quinlan**
emily.quinlan@commerce.nc.gov

▶ **Misty Herget**
misty.herget@commerce.nc.gov[115]

State FEMA Public Assistance Grant Support

The North Carolina Department of Public Safety's Division of Emergency Management (NCEM) maintains a list of contacts who might help with public assistance issues.[116] You may access the list here: https://www.ncdps.gov/our-organization/emergency-management /disaster-recovery/public-assistance.

State Hazard Mitigation Grant Support

Hazard Mitigation Disaster Grants Support at the North Carolina Department of Public Safety's Division of Emergency Management

▶ **Steve McGugan**
State Hazard Mitigation Officer
Steve.McGugan@ncdps.gov

▶ **Steven Jackson**
Deputy Hazard Mitigation Section Chief
Steven.Jackson@ncdps.gov

▶ **Jason Pleasant**
Development Supervisor
Jason.Pleasant@ncdps.gov

▶ **Kaine Riggan**
Infrastructure Lead
Kaine.Riggan@ncdps.gov

▶ **Portia Baldwin**
Grants Development Specialist
Portia.Baldwin@ncdps.gov

▶ **Jennifer Lewis**
Grants Development Specialist
Jennifer.Lewis@ncdps.gov[117]

---

113. Western NC Recovery Grants Program, https://www.deq.nc.gov/news/key-issues/storm -season/hurricane-helene-response/western-nc-recovery-grants-program (last visited May 13, 2026).

114. *Id.*

115. *Cf.* email from Maggie Battaglin to Taylor Morris (June 25, 2025, 07:44 PM EDT) (on file with the author) (discussing listing these four individuals as contacts).

116. Public Assistance, https://www.ncdps.gov/our-organization/emergency-management/disaster -recovery/public-assistance (last visited May 13, 2026) (navigate to the "Public Assistance Team Contact Information" section and expand the listings).

117. *See* Disaster Hazard Mitigation Grants, https://www.ncdps.gov/HMGP (last visited May 13, 2026) (listing these individuals as "Development Team Contacts").

Hazard Mitigation Non-Disaster Grants Support at the North Carolina Department of Public Safety's Division of Emergency Management

▶ **Kaine Riggan**
  Kaine.Riggan@ncdps.gov[118]

FEMA Contracting Reviews

FEMA may offer some review of solicitation documents or executed contracts that are intended to comply with FEMA standards. They may even be able to have a call with you to discuss your questions.

   To discuss accessing this potential service, email: fema-gpd-pdat@fema.dhs.gov.

School of Government Faculty

▶ **Rebecca Badgett**
  rbadgett@sog.unc.edu

Mutual Aid

"First Stop" Resources
▶ Your county and/or municipal attorney
▶ Your county and/or municipal emergency manager

Select Training

FEMA Emergency Management Institute Independent Study Training

These trainings are free and self-paced.[119] Users may receive a certificate of completion after passing the final exam for the training.[120] Taking the exam may require setting up a Student ID with FEMA.[121] More information on FEMA Student IDs can be found on the

---

118. *See* Non-Disaster Grants, https://www.ncdps.gov/our-organization/emergency-management/hazard-mitigation/non-disaster-grants (last visited May 13, 2026) (listing Kaine Riggan as a contact).

119. *See* Distance Learning, https://training.fema.gov/is/ (last visited May 13, 2026).

120. *See* Frequently Asked Questions (FAQs), https://training.fema.gov/is/isfaq.aspx (last visited May 13, 2026).

121. *See* Federal Emergency Management Agency Student Identification System, https://cdp.dhs.gov/femasid/#faq (last visited May 13, 2026) (expand the "Frequently Asked Questions" portion, which notes that "[a] FEMA SID [Student Identification] is required to register for and participate in any training provided by FEMA").

FEMA website: https://cdp.dhs.gov/femasid.[122] Readers can also see the entire independent study course list on the FEMA website: https://training.fema.gov/is/crslist.aspx.[123]

▶ **IS-706: NIMS Intrastate Mutual Aid—An Introduction***

Page with link to course and exam located here: https://training.fema.gov/is/courseoverview.aspx?code=IS-706

* Note that taking **IS-700.B: An Introduction to the National Incident Management System** is a prerequisite for this course.[124]

Page with link to that course and exam located here: https://training.fema.gov/is/courseoverview.aspx?code=IS-700.b

Select Publication

▶ **"Local Governments Assisting Other Local Governments During a Declared Disaster: Mutual Aid and Beyond"**

Coates' Canons post by Kara Millonzi

Available here: https://canons.sog.unc.edu/2024/10/local-governments-assisting-other-local-governments-during-a-declared-disaster/

Select Potentially Relevant Laws

▶ **G.S. 166A-19.72**

Emergency management mutual aid agreement authority

Available here: https://www.ncleg.gov/EnactedLegislation/Statutes/HTML/BySection/Chapter_166A/GS_166A-19.72.html

▶ **G.S. 58-83-1**

Local government firefighting mutual aid

Available here: https://www.ncleg.gov/EnactedLegislation/Statutes/HTML/ByArticle/Chapter_58/Article_83.html

▶ **G.S. 160A-288**

Municipal law enforcement cooperation

Available here: https://www.ncleg.gov/EnactedLegislation/Statutes/HTML/BySection/Chapter_160A/GS_160A-288.html

▶ **G.S. 153A-212**

County law enforcement cooperation

Available here: https://www.ncleg.gov/EnactedLegislation/Statutes/HTML/BySection/Chapter_153A/GS_153A-212.html

▶ **G.S. 160D-1107**

Local government building code administration and enforcement mutual aid agreements

Available here: https://www.ncleg.gov/EnactedLegislation/Statutes/HTML/BySection/Chapter_160D/GS_160D-1107.html

---

122. Federal Emergency Management Agency Student Identification System, https://cdp.dhs.gov/femasid (last visited May 13, 2026).

123. ISP Courses, https://training.fema.gov/is/crslist.aspx (last visited May 13, 2026).

124. *See* IS-706: NIMS Intrastate Mutual Aid—An Introduction, https://training.fema.gov/is/courseoverview.aspx?code=IS-706 (last visited May 13, 2026).

▶ **G.S. 160A-318**
Utility restoration mutual aid agreements
Available here: https://www.ncleg.gov/EnactedLegislation/Statutes/HTML/BySection/Chapter_160A/GS_160A-318.html

Other Miscellaneous Resources

NCWaterWARN Mutual Aid Agreement

Those interested in joining this agreement may visit the membership page on the NCWaterWARN website: https://www.ncwaterwarn.org/joinwaterwarn.html.[125] Users can explore the NCWaterWARN site to learn more about NCWaterWARN.[126]

Statewide Mutual Aid Agreement

Users can learn more about the agreement and how their local government unit can join on the North Carolina Department of Public Safety website: https://www.ncdps.gov/our-organization/emergency-management/em-operations/mutual-aid-north-carolina.[127]

State, Federal, Nonprofit, or Professional Organization Contact

Statewide Mutual Aid Agreement

For questions about the Statewide Mutual Aid Agreement, users can call North Carolina Emergency Management's (NCEM) Mutual Aid Coordinator at 919-621-4734 or email ncmutualaid@ncdps.gov.[128]

School of Government Faculty

▶ **Kara Millonzi**
millonzi@sog.unc.edu

---

125. Become a Member of NCWaterWARN Today!, https://www.ncwaterwarn.org/joinwaterwarn.html (last visited May 13, 2026).

126. *See, e.g.*, Frequently Asked Questions—NCWaterWARN, https://www.ncwaterwarn.org/faq.html (last visited May 13, 2026).

127. Mutual Aid in North Carolina, https://www.ncdps.gov/our-organization/emergency-management/em-operations/mutual-aid-north-carolina (last visited May 13, 2026).

128. *Id.*

Public Health

"First Stop" Resources
▶ Your local public health department
▶ Your county and/or municipal attorney
▶ Your county and/or municipal emergency manager

Select Trainings

FEMA Emergency Management Institute Independent Study Training

These trainings are free and self-paced.[129] Users may receive a certificate of completion after passing the final exam for the training.[130] Taking the exam may require setting up a Student ID with FEMA.[131] More information on FEMA Student IDs can be found on the FEMA website: https://cdp.dhs.gov/femasid.[132] Readers can also see the entire independent study course list on the FEMA website: https://training.fema.gov/is/crslist.aspx.[133]

▶ **IS-553.A: Coordination Between Water Utilities and Emergency Management Agencies**
Page with link to course and exam located here: https://training.fema.gov/is/courseoverview.aspx?code=IS-553.a

▶ **IS-1024: Water and Wastewater Treatment System Considerations**
Page with link to course and exam located here: https://training.fema.gov/is/courseoverview.aspx?code=IS-1024

Select Publications

Select North Carolina Department of Health and Human Services Publications

▶ **"Ensuring Water Safety After Hurricane Helene"**
North Carolina Department of Health and Human Services Division of Public Health blog post
Available here: https://www.dph.ncdhhs.gov/blog/2024/09/30/ensuring-water-safety-after-hurricane-helene

▶ **"Well and Septic Safety Following Hurricane Helene"**
North Carolina Department of Health and Human Services Division of Public Health blog post
Available here: https://www.dph.ncdhhs.gov/blog/2024/10/11/well-and-septic-safety-following-hurricane-helene

---

129. *See* Distance Learning, https://training.fema.gov/is/ (last visited May 13, 2026).

130. *See* Frequently Asked Questions (FAQs), https://training.fema.gov/is/isfaq.aspx (last visited May 13, 2026).

131. *See* Federal Emergency Management Agency Student Identification System, https://cdp.dhs.gov/femasid/#faq (last visited May 13, 2026) (expand the "Frequently Asked Questions" portion, which notes that "[a] FEMA SID [Student Identification] is required to register for and participate in any training provided by FEMA").

132. Federal Emergency Management Agency Student Identification System, https://cdp.dhs.gov/femasid (last visited May 13, 2026).

133. ISP Courses, https://training.fema.gov/is/crslist.aspx (last visited May 13, 2026).

Select School of Government Publications

▶ **"Can Counties and Cities Order 'Stay-at-Home'?"**

Coates' Canons post by Norma Houston (former School of Government faculty member)[134]

Available here: https://canons.sog.unc.edu/2020/03/can-counties-and-cities-order-shelter-in-place/

▶ **"Could Extreme Heat Cause a Legal Emergency Under North Carolina's Emergency Management Act?"**

Coates' Canons post by Taylor Morris

Available here: https://canons.sog.unc.edu/2025/05/could-extreme-heat-cause-a-legal-emergency-under-north
-carolinas-emergency-management-act/

▶ **"Why Declare a Local State of Emergency for Extreme Heat?"**

Coates' Canons post by Taylor Morris

Available here: https://canons.sog.unc.edu/2025/06/why-declare-a-local-state-of-emergency-for-extreme-heat/

○○○ Other Miscellaneous Resource

North Carolina Department of Health and Human Services On-Site Water Protection Branch Webpage

The North Carolina Department of Health and Human Services On-Site Water Protection Branch webpage may offer links to information and other resources helpful to local governments related to wastewater and wells for drinking water.[135] Users may navigate to links on the page to identify potential resources.[136] The webpage is available here: https://ehs.dph.ncdhhs.gov/oswp/.

 ## School of Government Faculty

▶ **Kirsten Leloudis**

kirsten@sog.unc.edu

▶ **Jill Moore**

moore@sog.unc.edu

---

134. *See* Faculty and Staff, https://www.sog.unc.edu/about/faculty-and-staff?page=1 (last visited May 13, 2026) (not including Norma Houston).

135. On-Site Water Protection Branch, https://ehs.dph.ncdhhs.gov/oswp/ (last visited May 13, 2026).

136. *See id.*

Public Meetings

"First Stop" Resources
- Your local government clerk's office
- Your local government attorney
- Your local government emergency manager

Select Publications

- **"Remote Meetings Still Up in the Air: Part 1"**
  Coates' Canons post by Kristina Wilson
  Available here: https://canons.sog.unc.edu/2025/05/remote-meetings-still-up-in-the-air-part-1/

- **"Remote Meetings Still Up in the Air: Part 2"**
  Coates' Canons post by Kristina Wilson
  Available here: https://canons.sog.unc.edu/2025/06/remote-meetings-still-up-in-the-air-part-2/

- **"Remote Meetings Still Up in the Air: Part 3"**
  Coates' Canons post by Kristina Wilson
  Available here: https://canons.sog.unc.edu/2025/09/remote-meetings-still-up-in-the-air-part-3/

- **"Can Appointed Boards Continue to Meet Remotely?"**
  Coates' Canons post by Kristina Wilson
  Available here: https://canons.sog.unc.edu/2022/08/can-appointed-boards-continue-to-meet-remotely/

- **"Misinformation and Threats in the Wake of Hurricane Helene: How Local Governments Can Respond—Part 2 (Public Meetings)"**
  Coates' Canons post by Kristina Wilson
  Available here: https://canons.sog.unc.edu/2024/10/misinformation-and-threats-in-the-wake-of-hurricane-helene-how-local-governments-can-respond-part-2-public-meetings/

- **"Public Meetings After the Lifting of the State-Level State of Emergency"**
  Coates' Canons post by Frayda Bluestein (former School of Government faculty member)[137]
  Available here: https://canons.sog.unc.edu/2021/07/public-meetings-after-the-lifting-of-the-state-level-state-of-emergency/

- **"Clarification of Rules for Remote Meetings Under State Level State of Emergency: No More Waiting 24 Hours After Public Hearings!"**
  Coates' Canons post by Frayda Bluestein (former School of Government faculty member)[138]
  Available here: https://canons.sog.unc.edu/2021/06/clarification-of-rules-for-remote-meetings-under-state-level-state-of-emergency-no-more-waiting-24-hours-after-public-hearings/

- **"Remote Zoning Hearings During Declared Emergencies"**
  Coates' Canons post by Adam Lovelady
  Available here: https://canons.sog.unc.edu/2020/05/remote-zoning-hearings-during-declared-emergencies/

---

137. *See* FACULTY AND STAFF, https://www.sog.unc.edu/about/faculty-and-staff (last visited May 13, 2026) (Frayda Bluestein no longer listed).

138. *See id.* (Frayda Bluestein no longer listed).

Select Potentially Relevant Law

▶ **G.S. 166A-19.24**

Remote meetings of public bodies under certain declared states of emergency
Available here: https://www.ncleg.gov/EnactedLegislation/Statutes/HTML/BySection/Chapter_166A/GS_166A-19.24.html

School of Government Faculty

▶ **Kristina Wilson**

wilson@sog.unc.edu

Utilities

"First Stop" Resources

▶ Your local government departments providing utilities
▶ Other local governments that provide utilities in your local government's jurisdiction
▶ Private companies that provide utilities in your local government
▶ Your county and/or municipal attorney
▶ Your county and/or municipal emergency manager

Select Trainings

FEMA Emergency Management Institute Independent Study Trainings

These trainings are free and self-paced.[139] Users may receive a certificate of completion after passing the final exam for the training.[140] Taking the exam may require setting up a Student ID with FEMA.[141] More information on FEMA Student IDs can be found on the FEMA website: https://cdp.dhs.gov/femasid.[142] Readers can also see the entire independent study course list on the FEMA website: https://training.fema.gov/is/crslist.aspx.[143]

▶ **IS-553.A: Coordination Between Water Utilities and Emergency Management Agencies**

Page with link to course and exam located here: https://training.fema.gov/is/courseoverview.aspx?code=IS-553.a

---

139. *See* Distance Learning, https://training.fema.gov/is/ (last visited May 13, 2026).

140. *See* Frequently Asked Questions (FAQs), https://training.fema.gov/is/isfaq.aspx (last visited May 13, 2026).

141. *See* Federal Emergency Management Agency Student Identification System, https://cdp.dhs.gov/femasid/#faq (last visited May 13, 2026) (expand the "Frequently Asked Questions" portion, which notes that "[a] FEMA SID [Student Identification] is required to register for and participate in any training provided by FEMA").

142. Federal Emergency Management Agency Student Identification System, https://cdp.dhs.gov/femasid (last visited May 13, 2026).

143. ISP Courses, https://training.fema.gov/is/crslist.aspx (last visited May 13, 2026).

▶ **IS-815: ABCs of Temporary Emergency Power**
Page with link to course and exam located here: https://training.fema.gov/is/courseoverview.aspx?code=IS-815

▶ **IS-860.C: The National Infrastructure Protection Plan, An Introduction**
Page with links to course and exam located here: https://training.fema.gov/is/courseoverview.aspx?code=IS-860.c

▶ **IS-913.A: Critical Infrastructure Security and Resilience: Achieving Results Through Partnership and Collaboration**
Page with links to course and exam located here: https://training.fema.gov/is/courseoverview.aspx?code=IS-913.a

▶ **IS-914: Surveillance Awareness: What You Can Do**
Page with links to course and exam located here: https://training.fema.gov/is/courseoverview.aspx?code=IS-914

▶ **IS-915: Protecting Critical Infrastructure Against Insider Threats**
Page with links to course and exam located here: https://training.fema.gov/is/courseoverview.aspx?code=IS-915

▶ **IS-916: Critical Infrastructure Security: Theft and Diversion—What You Can Do**
Page with links to course and exam located here: https://training.fema.gov/is/courseoverview.aspx?code=IS-916

▶ **IS-1024: Water and Wastewater Treatment System Considerations**
Page with link to course and exam located here: https://training.fema.gov/is/courseoverview.aspx?code=IS-1024

Select Publications

▶ **"Resuming Water and Wastewater Service After a Major Disruption"**
UNC-Chapel Hill School of Government Environmental Finance Center Blog post by Anna Patterson and Alicea Easthope-Frazer
Available here: https://efc.sog.unc.edu/resuming-water-and-wastewater-service-after-a-major-disruption/

▶ **"NCWaterWARN: What It Is and How to Access This Vital Resource"**
UNC-Chapel Hill School of Government Environmental Finance Center Blog post by Emma Copenhaver
Available here: https://efc.sog.unc.edu/ncwaterwarn-what-it-is-and-how-to-access-this-vital-resource/

▶ **"Financial Resiliency and Future Plans"**
Community and Economic Development in North Carolina and Beyond post by Carol Rosenfeld
Available here: https://ced.sog.unc.edu/2019/02/financial-resiliency-and-future-plans/

○○○ Other Miscellaneous Resources

NCWaterWARN Mutual Aid Agreement

Those interested in joining this agreement may go to the membership page on the NCWaterWARN website: https://www.ncwaterwarn.org/joinwaterwarn.html.[144] Users can explore the NCWaterWARN site to learn more about NCWaterWARN.[145]

---

144. BECOME A MEMBER OF NCWATERWARN TODAY!, https://www.ncwaterwarn.org/joinwaterwarn.html (last visited May 13, 2026).

145. *See, e.g.,* FREQUENTLY ASKED QUESTIONS—NCWATERWARN, https://www.ncwaterwarn.org/faq.html (last visited May 13, 2026).

UNC-Chapel Hill School of Government
Environmental Finance Center Technical Assistance

The Environmental Finance Center at UNC-Chapel Hill's School of Government may be able to offer free technical assistance to drinking water and wastewater systems.[146] These services may be available to systems outside of North Carolina but still in EPA Region 4, which also includes Alabama, Florida, Georgia, Kentucky, Mississippi, South Carolina, and Tennessee.[147]

Users can request technical assistance by filling out the Technical Assistance Request Form on the Environmental Finance Center website: https://efc.sog.unc.edu/technical-assistance/.[148]

School of Government Faculty

▶ **Kara Millonzi**
millonzi@sog.unc.edu

---

146. WHAT IS TECHNICAL ASSISTANCE?, https://efc.sog.unc.edu/technical-assistance/ (last visited May 13, 2026).

147. *Id.*

148. *Id.*